be free where you are

Other Parallax Press Books by Thich Nhat Hanh

Being Peace
Breathe! You Are Alive: Sutra on the Full Awareness of Breathing
Call Me by My True Names
Calming the Fearful Mind: A Zen Response to Terrorism
The Energy of Prayer: How to Deepen Your Spiritual Practice
Freedom Wherever We Go: A Buddhist Monastic Code for the Twenty-first Century
Finding Our True Home: Living the Pure Land Here and Now
The Heart of Understanding
Interbeing: Fourteen Guidelines for Engaged Buddhism
Keeping the Peace: Mindfulness and Public Service
Joyfully Together: The Art of Building a Harmonious Community
The Long Road Turns to Joy: A Guide to Walking Meditation
Old Path White Clouds: Walking in the Footsteps of the Buddha
Opening the Heart of the Cosmos: Insights on the Lotus Sutra
The Path of Emancipation
Peace Begins Here: Palestinians and Israelis Listening to Each Other
Plum Village Chanting and Recitation Book
Present Moment Wonderful Moment
The Sun My Heart: From Mindfulness to Insight Concentration
Teachings on Love
Touching Peace: Practicing the Art of Mindful Living
Touching the Earth: Intimate Conversations with the Buddha
Transformation and Healing: Sutra on the Four Establishments of Mindfulness
Understanding Our Mind

be free where you are

THICH NHAT HANH

Berkeley, California

Parallax Press
P.O. Box 7355
Berkeley, California 94707
www.parallax.org

Parallax Press is the publishing division
of Unified Buddhist Church, Inc.

Printed in the United States of America.

Calligraphy by Thich Nhat Hanh.
Author photograph by Nang Sao.
Cover and text design by Gopa & Ted2.

Thich Nhat Hanh is a Buddhist monk and social activist. He served as Chair of the Vietnamese Buddhist Peace Delegation to the Paris Peace Accords and was nominated by Dr. Martin Luther King, Jr. for the Nobel Peace Prize.

Library of Congress Cataloging-in-Publication Data
Nhat Hanh, Thich.
Be free where you are : a talk given at the Maryland Correctional Institution at Hagerstown / Thich Nhat Hanh.
p. cm.
ISBN 1-888375-23-X
1. Religious life—Buddhism. 2. Meditation (Buddhism) I. Title.
BQ5410 .N457 2001
294.3'444—dc21

13 / 14

Contents

Foreword

I accompanied Thây Thich Nhat Hanh to the Maryland Correctional Institution at Hagerstown on October 16th, 1999, along with Pritam Singh, Brother William, and many other friends. In order for us to join the more than one hundred inmates that were waiting for us in the chapel, we had to pass through sixteen checkpoints. At one gate, a security guard confiscated a small tape recorder that I was carrying with me to record Thây's talk. I stubbornly objected to his taking it from me, explaining to him that our teacher was getting old and I did not want to lose any of his Dharma talks. After a half an hour, he returned the recorder to me and we continued on. As it turns out, the correctional institution's recorder was not working, and it is thanks to my small tape recorder that this book, a transcription of the talk he gave to the inmates that day, is being made available to you.

During his talk, one of the things Thây

explained to the inmates was how to eat mindfully and joyfully in the present moment, with awareness of everyone and everything around us. When lunchtime came and we all sat down together, I was surprised to see that our inmate friends, even after hearing Thây's talk, still ate their food so quickly. Their habit energy was very strong. We had barely finished setting out the food for Thây when most of them had already finished their lunch! At first, I feared that they would not understand Thây's teaching about mindful eating. However, as we started to eat, our inmate friends began to watch us as we mindfully enjoyed our food. They could see the joy and mindfulness with which Thây picked up each morsel of food, as well as the friendly looks that we gave them from time to time. I hoped that after having had a chance to witness Thây embody his teaching while he ate, they too might enjoy eating more mindfully in the future.

Later that day, an inmate who had spent

thirty years in jail asked me what he could do to bring joy and peace into the world. Looking into his eyes, I could see that he was very sincere.

I turned to him and smiled. "One of the best things that you could offer to the people around you," I said, "is your way of being. You do not need to have money in your pocket or wait until you are out of jail to do something for the world. If you can practice dwelling peacefully in the present moment during the day, being mindful of whatever it is that you are doing, peace will radiate from you, and this will inspire the people around you.

"Perhaps there is an inmate or a guard who acts aggressively towards you. If you can look with compassion at him—with kindness and love—and offer him a gentle smile, he will be receiving something very precious from you. When you understand the pain of those who cause you suffering and choose to let it go, forgiveness will come naturally, because compassion will be present. When it is necessary, you can be firm and strong, but never lose your kindness or your beauty."

I knew that doing this would not be easy for him without a Sangha, so I suggested: "Why don't you form a small Sangha here? You can start by gathering two or three friends to discuss the practice that Thây has taught you today. Is it possible to do that during the religious service time?"

My friend's eyes grew brighter as he listened. "It will not be as easy as it sounds," he replied, "but I think it can be done."

Throughout the day the inmates showed a lot of interest in Thây's talk and asked many questions. I am quite sure the teachings and answers given to prisoners can be applied to any one of us — inside or outside the prison walls.

Sister Chân Không
March 3, 2002

be free
where
you are

For Warmth

Dear Friends, I wrote the following poem during the war in Vietnam after the town of Ben Tre was bombed by the United States Air Force. Ben Tre is the hometown of my colleague, Sister Chân Không. The U.S. forces destroyed the entire town because there were five or six guerrillas there. Later on, one officer declared that he had to bomb and destroy Ben Tre to save it from Communism. This poem is about anger.

I hold my face in my two hands.
No, I am not crying.
I hold my face in my two hands
to keep my loneliness warm—
two hands protecting,
two hands nourishing,
two hands preventing
my soul from leaving me
in anger.[1]

[1] See Thich Nhat Hanh, "For Warmth," in *Call Me by My True Names* (Berkeley: Parallax Press, 1999).

I was very angry. It was not just my anger, but the anger of a whole nation. Anger is a kind of energy that makes us and the people around us suffer. As a monk, when I get angry, I practice caring for my anger. I don't allow it to cause suffering or to destroy me. If you take care of your anger and are able to find relief, you will be able to live happily with much joy.

The Energy of Liberation

To take care of my anger I bring my attention to my breathing and look deeply inside myself. Right away I notice an energy there called anger. Then I recognize that I need another kind of energy to take care of this anger, and I invite that energy to come up to do that job. This second energy is called mindfulness. Every one of us has the seed of mindfulness within us. If we know how to touch that seed, we can begin to generate the energy of mindfulness, and with that energy, we can take good care of the energy of anger.

Mindfulness is a kind of energy that helps us to be aware of what is going on. Everyone is capable of being mindful. Those of us who practice daily have a greater capacity for being mindful than those who do not. Those who do not practice still have the seed of mindfulness, but its energy is very weak. By practicing just three days, the energy of mindfulness will already increase.

There can be mindfulness in anything you do. While you are drinking a cup of water, if you know that you are drinking water in that moment and you are not thinking of anything else, you are drinking mindfully. If you focus your whole being, body and mind, on the water, there is mindfulness and concentration, and the act of drinking may be described as mindful drinking. You drink not only with your mouth, but with your body and your consciousness, too. Everyone is capable of drinking his or her water mindfully. This is the way I was trained as a novice.

Walking mindfully is possible anywhere you are. When you walk, focus all your attention on the act of walking. Become aware of every step you take and don't think of anything else. This is called mindful walking. It is wonderfully effective. By doing this, you will begin to walk in such a way that every step brings you solidity, freedom, and dignity. You are the master of your own self.

Anytime I have to go from one place to another, I practice walking meditation—even if the distance is only five or six feet. Climbing up the stairs, I practice walking meditation. Going down the stairs, I practice walking meditation. Boarding an airplane, I practice walking meditation. Going from my room to the toilet, I practice walking meditation. Going to the kitchen, I practice walking meditation. I do not have any other style of walking—just mindful walking. It helps me very much. It brings me transformation, healing, and joy.

When you eat, you can practice mindfulness. Mindful eating can bring you a lot of joy and happiness. In my tradition, eating is a deep practice. First, we sit in a stable position and look at the food. Then, mindfully, we smile at it. We see the food as an ambassador that has come to us from the sky and from the Earth. Looking at a string bean, I can see a cloud floating in it. I can see the rain and the sunshine. I realize that this string bean is a part of the Earth and the sky.

When I bite into the string bean, I am aware that this is a string bean that I have put into my mouth. There is nothing else in my mouth—not my sorrow or my fear. When I chew the string bean, I am just chewing a string bean—not my worries or my anger. I chew very carefully, with one hundred percent of myself. I feel a connection to the sky, the Earth, the farmers who grow the food, and the people who cook it. Eating like this, I feel that solidity, freedom, and joy are possible. The meal not only nourishes my body, but also my soul, my consciousness, and my spirit.

Cultivating Freedom

For me, there is no happiness without freedom, and freedom is not given to us by anyone; we have to cultivate it ourselves. I will share with you how we get greater freedom for ourselves. During the time that we sit, walk, eat, or work outside, we cultivate our freedom. Freedom is what we practice every day.

No matter how or where you find yourself, if you have freedom, you are happy. I have many friends who spent time in forced labor camps and because they knew how to practice, they did not suffer as greatly. In fact, they grew in their spiritual lives, for which I am very proud of them.

By freedom I mean freedom from afflictions, from anger, and from despair. If you have anger in you, you have to transform anger in order to get your freedom back. If there is despair in you, you need to recognize that energy and not allow it to overwhelm you. You have to practice in such a way that you transform the energy of despair and attain the freedom you deserve —the freedom from despair.

You can practice freedom every moment of your daily life. Every step you take can help you reclaim your freedom. Every breath you take can help you develop and cultivate your freedom. When you eat, eat as a free person. When you walk, walk as a free person. When you breathe, breathe as a free person. This is possible anywhere.

By cultivating freedom for yourself, you will be able to help the people you live with. Even though you live in the same place, with the same physical and material conditions, if you practice, you will be a much freer person, a more solid person. Watching the way you walk, the way you sit, and the way you eat, people will be impressed. They will see that joy and happiness are possible for you, and will want to be like you because you are your own master, no longer a victim of anger, frustration, and despair. The practice that I have taken up as a Buddhist monk is the practice of freedom. When I became a novice, my teacher gave me a little book entitled *Stepping into Freedom: A Manual for a Novice Monk.*

To be able to breathe in and out is a miracle. A person on his or her deathbed cannot breathe freely, and he or she will soon stop breathing altogether. But I am alive. I can breathe in and become aware of my in-breath; I can breathe out and become aware of my out-breath. I smile at my out-breath and am aware that I am alive. So when you breathe in, be aware of your in-breath. "Breathing in, I know this is my in-breath." No one can prevent you from enjoying your in-breath. When you breathe out, be aware that this is your out-breath. Breathe as a free person.

For me, to be alive is a miracle. It is the greatest of all miracles. To feel that you are alive and are breathing in is to perform a miracle—one that you can perform at any time. Feeling that you are alive and that you are taking a step is a miracle. Master Linchi, a well-known meditation teacher who lived in the ninth century, said that the miracle is not walking on water but walking on the Earth.

Everyone walks on the Earth, but there are those who walk like slaves, with no freedom at all. They are sucked in by the future or by the past, and they are not capable of dwelling in the here and now, where life is available. If we get caught up in our worries, our despair, our regrets about the past, and our fears of the future in our everyday lives, we are not free people. We are not capable of establishing ourselves in the here and now.

Touching Miracles

According to the Buddha, my teacher, life is only available in the here and now. The past is already gone, and the future is yet to come. There is only one moment for me to live—the present moment. So the first thing I do is to go back to the present moment. By doing so, I touch life deeply. My in-breath is life, my out-breath is life. Each step I take is life. The air I breathe is life. I can touch the blue sky and the vegetation. I can hear the sound of the birds and the sound of another human being. If we can return to the here and now, we will be able to touch the many wonders of life that are available.

Many of us think that happiness is not possible in the present moment. Most of us believe that there are a few more conditions that need to be met before we can be happy. This is why we are sucked into the future and are not capable of being present in the here and now. This is why we step over many of the wonders of life. If we keep running away into the future, we cannot be in touch with the many wonders of life—we cannot be in the present moment where there is healing, transformation, and joy.

You Are a Miracle

When I eat an orange, I can eat the orange as an act of meditation. Holding the orange in the palm of my hand, I look at it mindfully. I take a long time to look at the orange with mindfulness. "Breathing in, there is an orange in my hand. Breathing out, I smile at the orange." For me, an orange is nothing less than a miracle. When I look at an orange in the here and now, I can see it with my spiritual eyes—the orange blossom, the sunshine and the rain going through the blossoms, the tiny green orange, and then the tree working over time to bring the orange to its full size. I look at the orange in my hand and I smile. It is nothing short of a miracle. Breathing in and out mindfully, I become fully present and fully alive, and now I see myself as a miracle.

Dear friends, you are nothing less than a miracle. There may be times when you feel that you are worthless. But you are nothing less than a miracle. The fact that you are here—alive and capable of breathing in and out—is ample proof that you are a miracle. One string bean contains the whole cosmos in it: sunshine, rain, the whole Earth, time, space, and consciousness. You also contain the whole cosmos.

We contain the Kingdom of God, the Pure Land of the Buddha, in every cell of our bodies. If we know how to live, the Kingdom of God will manifest for us in the here and now; with one step, we can penetrate it. We don't have to die to enter the Kingdom of God; in fact, we have to be very much alive. Hell, too, is in every cell of our body. It is up to us to choose. If we keep watering the seed of Hell in us each day, then Hell will be the reality we live in twenty-four hours a day. But if we know how to water the seed of the Kingdom of God in us each day, then the Kingdom of God will become the reality we live in every moment of our daily lives. This is my experience.

There is not a day I do not walk in the Kingdom of God. Whether I am in this place or somewhere else, I am always capable of walking mindfully, and the ground beneath my feet is always the Pure Land of the Buddha. No one can take that away from me. For me, the Kingdom of God is now or never. It is not situated in time or space; it is in our hearts. You have to develop mindful walking and touch the Earth as if it were a miracle. If you know how to go back to the here and now, if you know how to touch the Kingdom of God in every cell of your body, it will manifest to you right away in the here and now.

Freedom Is Possible Now

To touch the Kingdom of God, you need a little bit of training and a friend—a brother or a sister whose own practice can help you. When we see someone walking mindfully and enjoying every step he or she takes, we are motivated to go back to ourselves and do the same. A prisoner wrote to me in France saying that he had read my books and learned how to practice walking meditation in prison. He said he always walks up and down the stairs mindfully, and he enjoys every step he takes. Ever since he began this practice, his life has become pleasant. When he sees other inmates rushing up and down the stairs—with no stability or solidity, no calm or joy—he wishes they could learn to do walking meditation like him because every step he takes nourishes and transforms him.

Walk as a free person. Walk in such a way that every step brings you more dignity, freedom, and stability. Then joy and compassion will be born in your heart. You will realize that most other people do not walk like this, that they are possessed by their anger, their fear, and their despair. This may motivate you to help them learn how to live in the present moment, how to sit and walk as a free person does. One person sitting, walking, eating, and breathing as a free person can make an impact on the whole environment around him.

When I first came to the West, I was already practicing mindfulness. My purpose in coming here was to try to stop the destruction of human life in my country. I was just one person at that time. Everywhere I went, I practiced mindful walking and breathing, embodying the practice. As I made friends here, more and more people joined with me to call for an end to the atrocities being committed in Vietnam. Now I have tens of thousands of friends who practice mindfulness all over the world. Those who practice daily have been able to transform their lives and nourish their compassion and forgiveness. By doing this, they have been able to lessen the suffering of the people around them.

Walk As a Free Person

This morning when I stepped into the prison compound, I walked very mindfully. I noticed that the quality of the air was exactly like the quality of the air outside. When I looked at the sky, I saw that it was exactly the same as the sky outside. When I looked at the grass and the flowers, they too looked the same as the grass and flowers outside. Each step I took brought me the same kind of solidity and freedom that I experienced outside. So there is nothing that can prevent us from practicing successfully and bringing freedom and solidity to ourselves.

When you walk, breathe in; as you take two or three steps, call the name of someone you love, someone who can bring you a feeling of freshness, compassion, and love. With every step, call his or her name. Suppose I call the name of David. When I breathe in, I take two steps and quietly call, "David, David." When I call his name, David will be with me. I walk with peace and freedom so that David can walk with peace and freedom at the same time with me. When I breathe out, I take another two steps and say, "Here I am, here I am." So not only is David there for me, but I am there for him at the same time. "David, David. Here I am, here I am." I am entirely concentrated on the acts of walking and breathing. My mind is not thinking about anything else.

You can call to the Earth, "Earth, Earth. Here I am, here I am." The Earth is our mother and is always there for us. She has produced us, brought us to life; and she will receive us and bring us back again and again, countless times. So when I call, "Earth," I call to my awareness that is the ground of my being. "Here I am, here I am." If you practice like this for a few weeks or months, you will begin to feel much better.

The practice is to get in touch with elements inside ourselves that are wonderful, that refresh and heal us. Without mindfulness in our daily life, we tend to allow in many elements that are harmful to our bodies and our consciousnesses. The Buddha said that nothing can survive without food. Our joy cannot survive without food; neither can our sorrow or our despair.

If we have despair, it is because we have fed our despair the kind of food it thrives on. If we are depressed, the Buddha advises that we look deeply into the nature of our depression to identify the source of food that we use to nourish it. Once the source of the nutriments has been identified, cut it off. The depression will fade away after a week or two.

Without mindfulness in our daily lives, we feed our anger and despair by looking at or listening to things around us that are highly toxic. We consume many toxins each day; what we see on television or read in magazines can nourish our anger and despair. But if we breathe in and out mindfully and realize that these are not the kinds of things we want to consume, then we will stop consuming them. To live mindfully means to stop ingesting these kinds of poisons. Instead, choose to be in touch with what is wonderful, refreshing, and healing within yourself and around you.

Wonderful Moment

I have a breathing exercise that I would like to offer you. I'm sure that if you follow this exercise in difficult moments, you will find relief.

Breathing in, I know I am breathing in.
Breathing out, I know I am breathing out.
Breathing in, I notice that my in-breath
  has become deeper.
Breathing out, I notice that my out-
  breath has become slower.
Breathing in, I calm myself.
Breathing out, I feel at ease.
Breathing in, I smile.
Breathing out, I release.
Breathing in, I dwell in the present
  moment.
Breathing out, I feel it is a wonderful
  moment.

These verses can be summarized in the following way:

In, Out; Deep, Slow;
Calm, Ease; Smile, Release;
Present Moment, Wonderful Moment.

First we practice "In, Out." Breathing in, we say, "In," silently, in order to nourish the awareness that we are breathing in. When we breathe out, we say, "Out," aware that we are breathing out. Each word is a guide to help us return to our breathing in the present moment. We can repeat, "In, Out" until we find our concentration is peaceful and solid.

Then we say, "Deep" with the next in-breath and "Slow" with the next out-breath. When we breathe consciously, our breathing becomes deeper and slower, more peaceful and pleasant. We continue to breathe "Deep, Slow, Deep, Slow," until we want to move to the next phrase, which is "Calm, Ease."

"Calm" means we calm our body, we bring peace to our body. Breathing in, I bring the element of calm into my body. If we have a feeling or an emotion that makes us feel less peaceful, then calming means to calm that feeling or emotion. Breathing in, I calm my emotions. Breathing in, I calm my feelings. When we breathe out, we say, "Ease," which means being light, relaxed, feeling that nothing is as important as our well-being.

When we have mastered "Calm, Ease," we move to "Smile, Release." When we breathe in, even if we do not feel great joy at the moment, we can still smile. When we smile, our joy and peace become even more settled, and tension vanishes. When we breathe out, we say, "Release." We release what is making us suffer—an idea, a fear, a worry, anger.

And at last, we return to "Present Moment, Wonderful Moment." "Breathing in, I dwell in the present moment. Breathing out, I feel this is a wonderful moment." Remember, the Buddha said that the present moment is the only moment when life is available to us. So in order to touch life deeply, we have to come back to the present moment.

Our breath is like a bridge connecting our bodies and our minds. In our daily lives, our bodies may be in one place and our minds somewhere else—in the past or in the future. This is called a state of distraction. The breath is a connection between the body and the mind. When you begin to breathe in and out mindfully, your body will come back to your mind and your mind will go back to your body. You will be able to realize the oneness of body and mind and become fully present and fully alive in the here and now. You will be in a position to touch life deeply in the moment. This is not difficult. Everyone can do it.

Smiling As a Practice

In the exercise "Breathing in, I smile," you may ask: Why should I smile when there is no joy in me? The answer to that is: Smiling is a practice. There are over three hundred muscles in your face. When you are angry or fearful, these muscles tense up. The tension in these muscles creates a feeling of hardness. If you know how to breathe in and produce a smile, however, the tension will disappear—it is what I call "mouth yoga." Make smiling an exercise. Just breathe in and smile—the tension will disappear and you will feel much better.

There are times when your joy produces a smile. There are also times when a smile causes relaxation, calm, and joy. I do not wait until there is joy in me to smile; joy will come later. Sometimes when I am alone in my room in the dark, I practice smiling to myself. I do this to be kind to myself, to take good care of myself, to love myself. I know that if I cannot take care of myself, I cannot take care of anyone else.

Being compassionate to yourself is a very important practice. When you are tired, angry, or in despair, you should know how to go back to yourself and take care of your tiredness, your anger, and your despair. That is why we practice smiling, mindful walking and breathing, and mindful eating.

When You Feel Grateful, You Do Not Suffer

I notice that in the United States, where there is so much food and so many different kinds of things to eat, there is not much time to eat. Eating can be very joyful, and you don't need to eat a lot to be healthy.

When I pick up my food, whether it is with chopsticks or a fork, I take time to look at it for a moment. A fraction of a second is enough for me to identify the food. If I am really in the here and now, I will recognize the food right away, whether it is a carrot, a string bean, or bread. I smile at it, put it in my mouth, and chew it with complete awareness of what I am eating. Mindfulness is always mindfulness *of something,* and I chew my food in such a way that life, joy, solidity, and non-fear become possible. After twenty minutes of eating, I feel nourished—not only physically, but also mentally and spiritually. This is a very, very deep practice.

In Plum Village, we take time to eat. We eat as a community. Everyone sits beautifully and we wait for each other to begin together. When there is a brother or a sister eating mindfully on your right and on your left, you feel supported in the practice of eating mindfully. At the beginning of each meal, we practice the Five Contemplations.

The Five Contemplations

This food is the gift of the whole universe,
the Earth, the sky, and much hard work.
May we eat in such a way as to be worthy
to receive it.
May we transform our unskillful states
of mind and learn to eat in moderation.
May we take only food that nourishes
us and prevents illness.

We accept this food in order to realize
the path of understanding and love.

The First Contemplation is being aware that our food comes directly from the Earth and sky. It is a gift of the Earth and sky, and also of the people who cook it.

The Second Contemplation is about being worthy of the food we eat. The way to be worthy of our food is to eat mindfully—to be aware of its presence and thankful for having it. Take the string bean, for example. The Earth and sky have taken many months to produce a string bean. It is a pity to look at it and not see it as a miracle of life. The energy of mindfulness can help us to see how wonderful our food is while we are eating. We cannot allow ourselves to get lost in our worries, fears, or anger of the past or the future. We are there for the food because the food is there for us; it is only fair. Eat in mindfulness and you will be worthy of the Earth and the sky.

The Third Contemplation is about

becoming aware of our negative tendencies and not allowing them to carry us away. We need to learn how to eat in moderation, to eat the right amount of food. In Plum Village, each one of us has a bowl to eat from, and every time we serve ourselves, we know exactly how much we really need. The bowl that is used by a monk or a nun is referred to as an instrument of appropriate measure. It is very important not to overeat. If you eat slowly and chew very carefully, you will get plenty of nutrition. The right amount of food is the amount that helps us stay healthy.

The Fourth Contemplation is about the quality of our food. We are determined to ingest only food that has no toxins for our body and our consciousness. We promise to eat only the kinds of food that keep us healthy and nourish our compassion, and to avoid the kinds of food that contain or bring poisons into our body and make us less compassionate. This is mindful eating. The Buddha said that if you eat in such a way that compassion is destroyed in you, it is like eating the flesh of your own son or daughter. So practice eating in such a way that you can keep compassion alive in you.

The Fifth Contemplation is being aware that we receive food in order to realize something. Our lives should have meaning, and that meaning is to help people suffer less, help people touch the joys of life. When we have compassion in our hearts, when we know that we are able to help a person suffer less, life begins to have more meaning. This is very important food for us.

A single person is capable of helping many living beings. My colleague Sister Chân Không has been working with poor people, orphans, and the hungry for many years. She has helped thousands and thousands of people, and because of her work these people suffer less. This brings her a lot of joy and gives her life meaning. This can be true for all of us anytime, anywhere. Just saying a few words that make another person suffer less can give our lives meaning.

And it is something we can do anywhere.

When your life is meaningful, happiness becomes a reality and you become a *bodhisattva* right here and now. A bodhisattva is someone who has compassion within himself or herself and who is able to make another person smile or help someone suffer less. Every one of us is capable of this.

Compassion As a Liberating Factor

Every moment of your daily life can be a moment of practice. Whether you are waiting for your food or lining up to be counted, you can always practice breathing mindfully or practice smiling. Do not waste a moment of your daily life. Every moment is an opportunity to cultivate your solidity, peace, and joy. And after a few days, you will see people beginning to profit from your presence. Your presence can become the presence of a bodhisattva, a saint. It is possible.

There is a story that I read when I was seven years old. It was a Jataka story, which is a story about a former life of the Buddha. This story is about one of his lives before he became Buddha, when he was in Hell. The guard who was in charge of the inmates of Hell did not seem to have any compassion. He carried a big pitchfork, and every time anyone did something wrong, he would plunge the pitchfork into that person's chest. Although the inmates suffered greatly from their treatment, they could not die. That was their punishment: They suffered, but they did not die.

One day, the inmates were forced to carry heavy loads on their backs. The guard, with his pitchfork in hand, began to push them to go faster. The Buddha (in this previous incarnation) saw that one of the inmates could not keep up and that the guard was beginning to pick on him, threatening him with the pitchfork to make him move faster. At that moment, something was born in the Buddha. He wanted to intervene, to confront the guard even though he knew the guard would then turn on him. If his intervention would have resulted in his dying, he would have done it gladly. But the kind of punishment he could have expected in return would not have led to his death, only to more suffering. Even so, he courageously approached the guard and said, "Don't you have a heart? Why don't you give him time to carry his load?" Upon hearing this, the guard plunged the pitchfork into the chest of the Buddha, who died instantly and was born again as a human being.

It took courage for the Buddha to stand up and look the guard straight in the face for the sake of a fellow prisoner. He saw injustice, and as a result of so much suffering, compassion was born in his heart. His intervention was born from compassion. This was why he died right away and was born as a human being. From that time on, the Buddha began practicing until the time he became a fully enlightened person, a

Buddha. So even the Buddha, in one of his former lives, had hit the bottom of suffering. But thanks to the compassion born in his heart, he was able to liberate himself from his situation.

I have lived through a lot of suffering myself, and I can tell you that compassion can free you from the most difficult situations. It is the energy of compassion that helps us and provides us with a way out of difficult situations. There was a time when we brought boats into the Gulf of Siam to rescue boat people. Doing this work can be very dangerous because there are many pirates on the sea. But because we believed that the best means of self-protection was compassion, not violence, we never had guns on our boats while we were rescuing people; we only had compassion. According to the teaching and the practice I follow, compassion is the best means for self-protection.

In Buddhist circles, we speak about *Avalokiteshvara,* the bodhisattva of deep compassion and deep listening. The bodhisattva can manifest as a woman, a man, a child, a politician, or a slave, but the main characteristic of the bodhisattva is always the same—the presence of compassion in his or her heart. One time Avalokiteshvara manifested as a hungry ghost with a very ferocious face. He took on that appearance to help other hungry ghosts, but in truth, he was a compassionate being. Many of us are afraid of being attacked, so we sometimes pretend to be tough and cruel to protect ourselves, even though we have compassion and understanding inside. Without compassion, we suffer a lot and we make people around us suffer. With compassion, we can relate to other living beings and we can help them suffer less.

If you are inhabited by the energy of compassion, you live in the safest of environments. Compassion can be expressed in your eyes, in the way you act or react, in the way you walk, sit, eat, or deal with other people. It is the best means of self-protection. It can also be contagious. It is very wonderful to sit close to someone who has compassion in his or her heart. With compassion in your heart, you will win over a friend or two friends—because we all need compassion and love. Two people together can protect each other and those around them, too.

It is our practice to cultivate compassion in our daily lives. With the practice of compassion, we open to one person and then another, and finally, when compassion is present, any place can be a pleasant place to live. When the element of joy enters our bodies and consciousnesses, together we find peace and joy right here, right now.

Understanding Makes Compassion Possible

Understanding is the substance out of which we fabricate compassion. What kind of understanding am I talking about? It is the understanding that the other person suffers, too. When we suffer, we tend to believe that we are the victims of other people, that we are the only ones who suffer. That is not true—the other person also suffers. He has his difficulties, his fears, and his worries, too. If we could only see the pain within him, we would begin to understand him. Once understanding is present, compassion becomes possible.

Do we have enough time to look into the condition of the other person? The other person may be an inmate like us or a guard. If we look, we can see that there is a lot of suffering within him. Maybe he does not know how to handle his suffering. Maybe he allows his suffering to grow because he does not know how to handle it, and this makes him and other people around him suffer. So with this kind of awareness or mindfulness, you begin to understand, and understanding will give rise to your compassion. With compassion in you, you will suffer much less, and you will be motivated by a desire to do something—or not do something—so that the other person suffers less. Your way of looking or smiling at him may help him suffer less and give him faith in compassion.

I would describe my practice as the practice of cultivating compassion. But I know that compassion is not possible without understanding. And understanding is possible only if you have time to look deeply. Meditation means to look deeply in order to understand. In the monastery where I live, we have plenty of time to do the work of looking deeply. In a correctional house, there is also plenty of time and opportunity to practice looking deeply. It is a very good environment to practice looking deeply so that compassion can grow as a liberating factor. I think that if one, or ten, or twenty of you practice compassionate looking, you can transform this place in no time at all. You can bring paradise right here.

For me, paradise is a place where there is compassion. When there is compassion in your heart, you need only to breathe in and out and look deeply, and understanding will come. You will understand yourself and become compassionate toward yourself; you will know how to handle your suffering and take care of yourself. Then you will be able to help another person do the same, and compassion will grow between you. Thus, you become a Buddha, a bodhisattva who brings compassion into his environment and transforms Hell into Paradise. The Kingdom of God is now or never. This is very true. And it could be that you have more opportunities to practice than many of us. What do you think?

The Art of Handling a Storm

When a storm comes, it stays for some time, and then it goes. An emotion is like that too—it comes and stays for a while, and then it goes. An emotion is only an emotion. We are much, much more than an emotion. We don't die because of one emotion. So when you notice that an emotion is beginning to come up, it is very important that you put yourself in a stable sitting position, or you lie down, which is also a very stable position. Then focus your attention on your belly. Your head is like the top of a tree in a storm. I would not stay there. Bring your attention down to the trunk of the tree, where there is stability.

When you have focused on your belly, bring your attention down to the level just below the navel and begin to practice mindful breathing. Breathing in and breathing out deeply, be aware of the rise and fall of the abdomen. After practicing like this for ten, fifteen, or twenty minutes, you will see that you are strong—strong enough to withstand the storm. In this sitting or lying position, just stick to your breathing the way that someone on the ocean would stick to a life vest. After some time the emotion will pass.

This is a very effective practice, but please remember one thing: Don't wait until you have a strong emotion to practice. If you do, you will not remember how to practice. You have to practice now, today, while you are feeling fine, when you are not dealing with any strong emotions. This is the time to begin learning the practice. You can practice for ten minutes every day. Sit and practice breathing in and out, focusing your attention on your belly. If you do this for three weeks—twenty-one days—it will become a habit. Then when anger rises up or you are overwhelmed by despair, you will naturally remember the practice. Once you succeed, you will have faith in the practice and you will be able to tell your emotion, "Well, if you come again, I will do exactly the same thing." You will not be afraid because you know what to do.

Practice regularly. Once your practice becomes a habit, you will feel as though you are missing something when you don't do it. It will bring you well-being and stability. It will have a good effect on your health as well. This is the best kind of protection you can offer yourself. I always think that the energy of mindfulness is the energy of the Buddha, the energy of God, the Holy Spirit, that is inside of us protecting us all the time. Every time you touch the seed of mindfulness and practice mindful breathing, the energy of God, the energy of the Buddha, is there to protect you.

When you learn the practice, you may like to tell a friend, a relative, or your children, if you have any, how to practice. I know mothers who practice with their children. They hold their child's hand and say, "Darling, breathe with me. Breathing in, I am aware that my abdomen is rising. Breathing out, I am aware that my abdomen is falling." They guide their child to breathe with them until he or she gets through the emotion.

If you know the practice, you will be able to generate the energy of stability, and you will be able to hold another person's hand and transmit to him or her the energy of your stability. You can help that person cross out of the eye of the storm; it may help save someone's life. So many young people these days don't know how to handle their emotions. The number of people who commit suicide is enormous. This is a simple exercise, but very important.

Smile at Your Habit Energy

There is a strong energy in every one of us called habit energy. *Vasana* is the Sanskrit word for habit energy. Every one of us has habit energies that push us to say and do things we don't want to say or do. These habit energies damage us and our relationships to other people. Intellectually we know that saying or doing a certain thing will cause a lot of suffering, and yet we still say or do it. And once you say or do something, the damage is done. Then you regret it. You beat your chest and pull your hair. You say, "I am not going to say or do that thing again." But though you say this with sincerity, the next time the situation presents itself, you say and do the same thing. This is the power of habit energy that your parents and ancestors may have transmitted to you.

Mindful breathing can help you recognize habit energy when it emerges. You don't have to fight that energy; you only have to recognize it as yours and smile at it. That is enough. "Hello there, my habit energy. I know you're there, but you cannot do anything to me." You smile at it, and then you are free. This is a wonderful protection. It is why I said mindfulness is the energy of God, the energy of the Buddha protecting us.

In order for the energy of mindfulness to work for you, it is very important that you practice mindful walking and mindful breathing each day. When the habit energy begins to manifest, continue to breathe, recognize it, and say, "Hello, my habit energy. I know you are there, but I am free. You are not going to push me to say and do those things again." This is how you acquire a different way of reacting—you create a good habit energy to replace the bad habit energy.

Our relationships with other people are crucial to our happiness. Sometimes we treat others or ourselves badly because of habit energy. We should treat ourselves with respect, tenderness, and compassion. This is very important. If we know how to treat our bodies and feelings with respect, we will be able to treat other people with the same respect. This is the way we create peace, freedom, and happiness in the world. Every one of us is capable of doing this. We only need a little training. To have a friend who knows the practice is fortunate. With two people practicing, you can support each other in the practice of cultivating that energy called mindfulness—mindfulness of walking, mindfulness of breathing, mindfulness of eating.

Every moment of our daily lives can be used to cultivate mindfulness—the energy of the Buddha, the Holy Spirit. Wherever the Holy Spirit is, there is understanding, forgiveness, and compassion. The energy of mindfulness has the same nature. If you know how to generate this energy, you become truly present, truly alive, and you become capable of understanding. With understanding you will become compassionate, and that will change everything.

Questions and Answers

If you have any questions concerning the daily practice of mindfulness, I will be very happy to offer answers to them now.

Q: Have you ever been mad? When was the last time you were mad?

A: As a human being I have the seed of anger in me, but thanks to the practice, I am able to handle my anger. If anger manifests in me, I know how to take care of it. I am not a saint, but because I know the practice, I am no longer a victim of my anger.

Q: How long does it take to become successful in the practice?

A: It is not a matter of time. If you do it correctly and with pleasure, you can realize success quickly. However, if you take a lot of time and do not do it correctly, you may not realize anything. It is like mindful breathing. If you do it correctly, the first in-breath can bring you some relief and joy. But if you don't do it correctly, three or four hours will not bring you the desired effect. It is good to have a friend, a brother or a sister who is successful in the practice, to help and sup port you.

You can also do it alone. When you breathe in, allow yourself to breathe in naturally. Focus all your attention on the in-breath. When you breathe out, allow yourself to breathe out normally. Just become aware of your out-breath; don't interfere with it. Don't use force. If you allow yourself to breathe in and out natu rally and become aware of your breath, there will be improvement in only fifteen or twenty seconds. You will begin to feel pleasure in breathing in and out.

I once held a retreat in Montréal, Canada. After the first session of walking meditation, a lady came to me and asked, "Thây, can you authorize me to share the practice of walking meditation with other people?" In the seven years since she had come to this country, she had not been able to walk with as much serenity and peace as she experienced after just one session of walking meditation at the retreat. It was so healing, so refreshing for her that she wanted to share this practice of mindful walking with her friends. I said, "Why not?" She is proof that after one hour of walking meditation, a person is able to find relief and joy. But it is not to be measured by time. Whether it is mindful breathing, mindful walking, mindful eating, or mindful working, when you feel the effect right away and when the practice is pleasant, the practice is correct.

Q: How much time should I give to the practice?

A: The kind of meditation that I advocate can be done anytime. While you walk from one place to another, you can apply the techniques of mindful walking. When you do your work, you can practice mindful working. When you eat lunch, you can practice mindful eating. You don't have to set up a specific time to practice; it can be done at any time of the day.

If the situation permits, however, you can set aside time to do specific things, like waking up fifteen minutes earlier so that you can enjoy fifteen minutes of sitting meditation. Or before going to sleep—even after the lights have been turned off—you can sit on your bed to do fifteen minutes of mindful breathing. Because there are things you have to do collectively with other people, you may not be able to find a specific time to do what you want to do. So it will depend on how creative you can be with your time. But remember, the practice is available to you at any time, even when you go to urinate or while you are washing the floors.

You can scrub the floor as a free person or as a slave. That is up to you. Here, everyone has to do certain things, but you can do them as a free person. You can cultivate your freedom. This brings a lot of dignity, and everyone will sense it. With the practice, you are really free, no matter what situation you find yourself in.

I propose that every time you go to the toilet—every time you defecate, urinate, and wash your hands—you invest one hundred percent of yourself in the act. Stop all thinking; just enjoy doing it. It can be very pleasant. In a few weeks, you will see the wonderful effect of this practice.

Q: Can you define mindfulness? How can we practice with so many distractions?

A: In Vietnamese, "mindfulness" is *chanh niem,* which means to be truly present in the moment. When you eat, you know that you are eating. When you walk, you know that you are walking. The opposite of mindfulness is forgetfulness. You eat but you don't know that you are eating, because your mind is elsewhere. When you bring your mind back to what is happening in the here and now, that is mindfulness, and mindfulness can bring you a lot of life, pleasure, and joy. The simple act of eating an orange, for instance, can be a thousand times more pleasant if you eat it mindfully than if you eat it while you are caught up in your worries, anger, or despair. So mindfulness is the energy that helps you be fully present with whatever is there.

Suppose you hear noises in your surroundings. You can use noise as the object of mindfulness. "Breathing in, I can hear a lot of noise. Breathing out, I smile at this noise. I know that people making noise are not always peaceful, and I feel compassion toward them." So practicing mindful breathing and using the suffering that is around you as the object of your mindfulness will help the energies of understanding and compassion arise in you.

At a retreat, a woman complained that her roommate's snoring did not allow her to sleep. She was about to take her sleeping bag and go to the meditation hall when she suddenly remembered what I had taught, and she decided to stay. She used the sound as a bell of mindfulness to engender compassion. “Breathing in, I am aware of the snoring. Breathing out, I smile at it.” Ten minutes later, she was sound asleep. It was a wonderful discovery for her.

Q: Could you speak a little bit about forgiveness?

A: Forgiveness is the fruit of understanding. Sometimes even when we want to forgive someone, we cannot. The goodwill to forgive may be there, but the bitterness and suffering are still there, too. For me, forgiveness is the result of looking deeply and understanding.

One morning, in the office we had in Paris during the seventies and eighties, we received very bad news. A letter came saying that an eleven-year-old girl, a passenger on a boat leaving Vietnam, had been raped by a sea pirate. When her father tried to intervene, they threw him into the ocean. So the little girl jumped into the ocean too, and drowned. I was angry. As a human being, you have the right to get angry; but as a practitioner, you do not have the right to stop practicing.

I could not eat my breakfast; the news was too much for me. I practiced walking meditation in the woods nearby. I tried to get in touch with the trees, the birds, and the blue sky in order to calm myself, and then I sat down and meditated. The meditation lasted quite a long time.

During the meditation, I saw myself born as a baby in the coastal area of Thailand. My father was a poor fisherman, my mother was a woman without education. There was poverty all around me. When I was fourteen, I had to work with my father on the fishing boat to earn our living; it was very hard work. When my father died, I had to take over the business by myself to support the family.

A fisherman I knew told me that a lot of boat people coming out of Vietnam often carried their valuables, like gold and jewelry, with them. He suggested that if we intercepted just one of these boats and took some of the gold, we would be rich. Being a poor, young fisherman with no education, I was tempted. And one day, I decided to go with him to rob the boat people. When I saw the fisherman rape a female on the boat, I was tempted to do that, too. I looked around, and when I saw there was nothing to stop me—no police, no threat—I said to myself, "I can do it, too, just once." That is how I became a sea pirate raping a little girl.

Now suppose you are on the boat and you have a gun. If you shoot me and kill me, your act will not help me. In all my life, no one helped me, and in all their lives, no one helped my father or my mother. As a little boy, I was raised without an education. I played with delinquent children, and grew up to become a poor fisherman. No politician or educator ever helped me. And because no one helped me, I became a sea pirate. If you shoot me, I will die.

That night I meditated on this. Once

again I saw myself as a young fisherman becoming a sea pirate. I also saw a few hundred babies being born that night all along the coastline of Thailand. I realized that if no one helped these babies to grow up with an education and with an opportunity to lead a decent life, in twenty years some of these babies would be sea pirates. I began to understand that if I had been born as a little boy in that fishing village, I too might have become a sea pirate. When I understood that, my anger toward the pirates melted.

Instead of getting angry at the fisherman, I felt compassion toward him. I vowed if I could do anything to help the babies that had been born that night along the coast of Thailand, I would help. The energy called anger was transformed into the energy of compassion through meditation. Forgiveness cannot be obtained without that sort of understanding, and understanding is the fruit of looking deeply, which I call meditation.

Q: What is the essence of Buddhism? Is it

a religion? And was Buddha a god?

A: The Buddha always reminds us that he is a human being, not a god. He is a teacher. He left behind many discourses that he gave to his disciples. They are called sutras. This morning I offered you the practice of mindful breathing. This comes from the sutra called the *Discourse on Mindful Breathing*. In this text, he offers sixteen exercises of mindful breathing to deal with the difficulties in our daily lives, to cultivate wisdom, compassion, and so on. There are other discourses on the practice of mindfulness that lead to transformation and healing. They are not prayers; they are texts that teach you how to deal with suffering and difficulties in your daily life.

Buddhism originally was not a religion; it was a way of life. The sutras are the teachings of the Buddha on how to transform suffering and cultivate joy and compassion. As Buddhist monks, we learn many of these sutras, and we learn how to explain them to people in a way that they know exactly how to practice these teachings.

In the Buddhist tradition, we honor the Three Jewels. The First Jewel is the Buddha, the one who found a way of understanding, love, transformation, and healing. The Second Jewel is the Dharma, the path of transformation and healing, which was offered by the Buddha in the form of discourses, teachings, and practices. The Third Jewel is the community of practice, the Sangha—the men and women who have formed a community and taken up the path of meditation and mindfulness practice.

Sangha means "community." Everyone in the community practices mindful breathing, mindful walking, and generating compassion and understanding. It is our practice to take refuge in the Sangha because a real Sangha is a community where true practice exists—true mindfulness, understanding, and compassion. A true Sangha carries within itself the true Dharma and the true Buddha. So when you get in touch with a true

Sangha, you also get in touch with the Buddha and the Dharma.

With a Sangha, you have a chance to succeed, because the Sangha is instrumental in protecting and supporting you in the practice. Without a Sangha, you might abandon your practice after a few months. We have a saying that when a tiger leaves the mountain to go to the lowland, it will be captured by humans and killed. A practitioner must stay with his or her Sangha or he or she may abandon the practice after a few months. The support and guidance given by the Sangha are very important.

Even here, you can set up your own Sangha of four or five people who do the practice daily—mindful walking, breathing, eating, and working. A Sangha can give the support that is needed. A Sangha can be made up of laypeople or monastics, but wherever there are at least four people who practice mindfulness together, there is a Sangha. Taking refuge in the Sangha is very important. If the Sangha really practices, it contains the Buddha and the Dharma within it.

Q: What is mindfulness and what can it bring about?

A: Mindfulness, as I have said, is the capacity of being present in the here and now. Focus your attention on what is going on. If mindfulness is there, concentration will be there, too. If you continue to be mindful of something, then you will concentrate on it; it will become the object of your concentration. When your mindfulness and concentration are good, you will be able to receive insights; you will begin to understand in depth what is really happening in the here and now. So the process is mindfulness, concentration, and insight. The insight helps you to understand, and it liberates you from your wrong perceptions. It makes you stop suffering.

Q: Can we think of the past and plan for the future?

A: Mindfulness means to establish yourself in the present moment. But that does not mean you don't have the right to scrutinize and learn from the past or plan for the future. If you are really grounded in the present moment and the future becomes the object of your mindfulness, you can look deeply at the future to see what you can do in the present moment for such a future to become possible. We say that the best way of taking care of the future is to take care of the present, because the future is made of the present. Taking care of the present moment is one of the best things you can do in order to ensure a good future.

When we bring past events to the present moment and make them the object of our mindfulness, it teaches us a lot. When we were part of those events, we could not see them as clearly as we do now. With the practice of mindfulness, we have new eyes, and we can learn many things from the past.

Q: Please say a little more about breathing.

A: The quality of breathing improves with your practice. Your breath becomes deeper and slower. It brings more pleasure into your body and consciousness, and yet, everything else is the same. As you continue to breathe, walk, and sit as you normally do, the quality of your breathing, walking, and sitting improves. The practice of conscious breathing should bring you more pleasure, life, and joy. Nothing negative should come out of the practice of meditation; if we experience qualities opposite to those of peace, relaxation, and joy, there is something wrong. Meditation should only increase our quality of life in the present moment.

Q: I think in the West the emphasis is on being successful. Is there such a thing as success?

A: Take walking meditation as an example. We may do walking meditation for a while, enjoying every step. Then because we like looking at things such as trees, rocks, clouds, etc., we spot a very beautiful flower in front of us and we want to stop our walking meditation and contemplate its beauty. There is nothing wrong with this, because even when we stop walking, our enjoyment continues.

The same is true with meditation. While you are enjoying your in-breath and out-breath, an idea may suddenly come to you. You have the freedom to choose to continue with your mindful breathing or to stay with the idea. You can decide to say to your idea, "I would like to continue with my mindful breathing before I spend time with you." If that idea accepts your decision, it will recede into the background so you can continue your meditation. It is like looking through a pile of letters on your desk and setting a special letter aside to read last.

Mindfulness can be mindfulness of anything you like in the present moment. What if the idea is very strong and wants your attention right away? Then you can say,

"Okay, I'll stop focusing on my breathing now and pay attention to you." Then you can decide to focus all your attention on this new object of meditation. There is no harm in this.

If during sitting meditation you begin to feel some pain in your legs after just ten minutes, you may think that you have to bear the pain and sit for the entire fifteen minutes; otherwise you will have failed. You do not have to feel this way. You can practice mindful massaging instead. "Breathing in, I know that I am starting to change my sitting position. Breathing out, I smile at my muscle pain." You are free to choose the object of your mindfulness. You have not abandoned meditation. Not one second of your meditation has been lost. You have not failed.

Q: What is a Zen master?

A: A Zen master is someone who has practiced Zen meditation for some time, has acquired some experience, and is capable of sharing this practice with other people.

Q: I have a Christian background. Is it okay if I practice mindfulness?

A: I have studied Christianity and I have found many teachings on mindfulness in Christianity, and also in Judaism and Islam. I think that mindfulness has a universal nature. You can find it in every spiritual tradition. If you study deeply the life of a sage from any tradition, you will find a quality of mindfulness in his or her life. A sage is capable of living every moment of his or her life deeply and of touching the beauty and truth in each moment of life.

I think it is possible to profit from many traditions at the same time. If you love oranges, you are welcome to eat them, but nothing prevents you from enjoying kiwis or mangoes as well. Why commit yourself to only one kind of fruit when the whole spiritual heritage of humankind is available to you? It is possible to have Buddhist roots as well as Christian or Jewish roots. We grow very strong that way.

Q: Is there a kind of force that directs your existence? Is there a higher force that gives you direction?

A: I have said that in every cell of your body, you can find both Heaven and Hell. The higher or lower spiritual force is right there inside of you. When you have compassion, you can touch compassion everywhere. When you have violence and hatred, you will connect with those energies around you. This is why it is very important to select the channel you want to be on.

If you decide to nourish yourself with positive energies only, then the energy of mindfulness will help you distinguish between energies that are appropriate for you and those that are not—which people you should associate with, what kind of food you should eat, what kind of television programs you should watch, and so on. Mindfulness is capable of telling you things you need and things that are harmful to you.

Q: Would you explain something about your poetry?

A: My poetry is something that happens throughout the day. When I water the vegetables or wash dishes, poetry is born in me. When I sit down at the writing table, all I do is deliver the poems. Poetry comes as an inspiration and is the fruit of my mindful living. After a poem is born, I may realize that it helped me. The poem is like a "bell of mindfulness."

Sometimes you need to reread a poem you have written because it takes you back to a wonderful experience—it reminds you of the beauty available inside of you and all around you. So a poem is a flower you offer to the world, and at the same time, it is a bell of mindfulness for you to remember the presence of beauty in your daily life.

Appendix

The following are comments written by a few of those who attended the talk given by Thich Nhat Hanh on October 16, 1999 at the Maryland Correctional Institution at Hagerstown (MCIH).

Impressions of Thich Nhat Hanh

I watched in amazement as a tiny man, Thich Nhat Hanh, gracefully walked onto the stage at the Maryland Correctional Institution in Hagerstown and sat down crosslegged. I was amazed because there were some eighty guests from all over the United States and the world, and more than one hundred and twenty restless prisoners all sitting in the auditorium waiting for the appearance of this man, and he ignored all of us.

He sat down in mindful meditation, although we did not know this at first. He sat in peace and repose, oblivious to the noise and confusion of staff scurrying around to place amplification equipment, oblivious to the whispers and murmuring of the audience, and oblivious to the ministrations of his entourage. And frankly, many people just stared. How could he sit there so blissfully? How could the guest of honor ignore us? His face was calm and remarkably unlined. He just sat there.

And we reacted to his peace before he even said a word. The staff tested the audio until satisfied and then left the equipment in place and exited the stage, the echoes from their feet on the hardwood floors finally silent. The murmuring in the room gradually got lower and lower, and ceased. His entourage became satisfied that the scatter rugs and blankets were properly positioned on the stage, and settled themselves into their own mindful meditation.

And before he ever opened his mouth, he had our rapt attention. We wanted what he had. And as a result, the Maryland Correctional Institution Weekly prisoner newsletter just reported the implementation of a new meditation program! Amazing impact from a humble man who began by ignoring his audience.

Douglas Scott Arey
MCIH

. . . . Thich Nhat Hanh's comments, advice, and sincere belief in what he explains and practices have changed a lot of lives in here. He is now thousands of miles from the Maryland Correctional Institution in Hagerstown, but his talk penetrated the hearts of hundreds who were in this prison and gave wings to us for flight to a land where wisdom and understanding is the passport and forgiveness is the visa.

Ahmad Nowrouzi
MCIH

. . . . We applaud MCIH for bringing this holy man to his first American prison. So many of us, inmates and outsiders alike, are in prisons of our own making, prisons made up of resentment against those who have hurt us and a desire for revenge. The miracle of mindfulness can free us all.

Shepherdstown Chronicle (12/03/99)
"Some Things Considered"
by Donna Acquaviva

The prison environment is simultaneously one of the most crucial places for one to have a strong spiritual practice, and one of the most difficult places for it to bloom and sustain itself. Having worked in prisons for thirty years, I am truly thrilled to see Dharma-elders such as Thich Nhat Hanh speaking directly to prisoners about both the importance and difficulties of such practice. Prisoners need books such as this one, and we on the outside need the prisoners' own example of right effort and dedication to inspire us in meeting our own challenges. May Dharma and Compassion continue to break down the walls from both sides, so that we may see through the formidable differences in our environments and backgrounds to the eternal unity we share in the refuge of our essential Nature.

Bo Lozoff
Director and Co-founder
Human Kindness Foundation

Help the Parallax Press Prison Project

Parallax Press welcomes contributions to the Prison Project to fulfill the numerous requests we receive from incarcerated individuals or prison libraries requesting free copies of our publications.

Prison Project
Parallax Press
P.O. Box 7355
Berkeley, CA 94707
prisonproject@parallax.org

Parallax Press, a nonprofit organization, publishes books on engaged Buddhism and the practice of mindfulness by Thich Nhat Hanh and other authors. For a copy of our free catalog, please contact:

Parallax Press
P.O. Box 7355
Berkeley, CA 94707
Tel: (510) 525-0101
www.parallax.org

Monastics and laypeople practice the art of mindful living in the tradition of Thich Nhat Hanh at retreat communities in France and the United States. To reach any of these communities, or for information about individuals and families joining for a practice period, please contact:

Plum Village
13 Martineau
33580 Dieulivol, France
www.plumvillage.org

Blue Cliff Monastery
3 Mindfulness Road
Pine Bush, NY 12566
www.bluecliffmonastery.org

Deer Park Monastery
2499 Melru Lane
Escondido, CA 92026
www.deerparkmonastery.org